BOOK SIGNINGS FOR ABSOLUTE BEGINNERS

THE QUESTIONS NEW AUTHORS ARE TOO EMBARRASSED TO ASK EXPERIENCED SIGNERS

CIARA CAVE

Copyright © 2017 by Ciara Cave

All rights reserved.

No part of this book may be reproduced in any form or by any electronic or mechanical means, including information storage and retrieval systems, without written permission from the author, except for the use of brief quotations in a book review and the packing list to be found on the final page.

ISBN: 9780648120544

Thanks so much to my family—the world's best husband and my daughters, Gal & Ted plus Cocoa Bean. Also to the friends who really are family, including Tracey, Suzi & Sassie...
You chicks rock!

FOREWORD

Please be aware this book is prepared and written in Australian English. Spelling etc., will be using the *"ise"* versus *"ize"* spelling. *This is not a typographical error.*

Throughout the book I will preface a range of sites (in an Australian context) that I use to purchase items for signings. This is not a all there are, simply a beginning point and focussed on where you can purchase these items in Australia and New Zealand. A quick google search will bring up a range of websites that will offer information for the country in which you live as will chatting with authors in your area.

Do remember if you are purchasing items from overseas to check that they are legal, do not contain dangerous additives and to allow for shipping costs and time.

Further versions of this title **may** include lists of country specific websites but I make no guarantees that this will happen in the foreseeable future.

This book is not a comprehensive how-to, but simply put a book that will help you to make decisions on how best to go forward and prepare for your first book signings as an author.

I hope this book helps you to overcome those first signing nerves and you sell a heap of copies of your title!

Ciara Cave

aka Imogene Nix

1 / THE EXPRESSION OF INTEREST

I HAVE a friend who is currently in the process of organising a signing and she's gone to the trouble of creating an EOI (Expression Of Interest Form) and while it's not a huge thing to fill in the form there are some basic steps all authors should step through.

1. Read the form before you fill it out. Gather the information required, because it will make your life easier.

2. Filling in the form with your legal name: from time to you will be asked for this information. The organiser isn't being nosy, make sure you add this information as it could be necessary for legal purposes.

3. Check your URL's are correct: if you're giving a Facebook URL make sure it's the right one and the organiser ends up with someone else's page and can't see your an author.

4. Amazon URL: to be honest, not everyone has one but if the organiser is asking for one, they want to see the books you're likely to be taking to the event. It could be to check that you meet their criteria. If you don't have one yet,

contact the organiser and check as they may give you an alternatively link to give.

Here is a working example:

Full url: https://www.amazon.com/Imogene-Nix/e/B0073P6YW8/ref=sr_ntt_srch_lnk_1?qid=1504054765&sr=8-1 (incredibly messy.)

There is a point at which you can shorten this link to this:

https://www.amazon.com/Imogene-Nix/e/B0073P6YW8/

4. Payment - make sure you pay in a timely fashion, because a lot of these events have a capped number of authors and if you don't get that payment in by the due date, your spot could be lost!

Fill in everything you possibly can to ensure that you're accepted to the signing.

> Expressions of Interest do not mean that you definitely have a spot, they are simply saying you are interested in attending. It is only after you get the acceptance or invitation that you are assured a spot.

2 / BEGINNING TO PREPARE

As a somewhat experienced book signing attendee/author, I get asked a lot about what is needed for the large signing events at hotels/convention centres etc.,

Personally, I carry a range of items & stock for signings. I also have a set-up that allows for readers to gain the most out of my signing experiences.

So, where do we start? Usually, when you sign-up to conventions etc., the organisers now begin with a Facebook page or group. It is highly recommended that if you are participating and there is one, get in and get on regularly. The more readers know your name and the more you interact the better your chances they will feel they simply must buy your book.

I would also suggest preparing a "Pre-Order" form. This can be done easily through either your website or using google forms.

http://forms.google.com

Simply ensure you have a google account and you have access to the email address you use for sending the individual responses to you.

I would also suggest it is important to Preview your form and have someone check it over for typos etc before you make it available to the general public.

Take some time and get to know your organisers and those other authors who are attending. Many are in the same boat as you and there's nothing worse than trying to feel your way through the planning and set-up and feeling terribly alone. Remember, if you feel like that, so will many others.

> CONSIDER: if you have the opportunity to discount your books for the signing—making the price competitive can sometimes be the difference between sitting there and feeling unloved and selling bucketloads of books.

3 / ACCEPTING CARDS

It is always recommended that you ensure there are multiple ways for your readers to pay for your books.

Do you sticker your books or have a sign? I prefer a sign because it doesn't mess up my books, but it's authors choice.

The easier it is for them to complete their orders, the more they are likely to purchase from you. To that end, you need to consider:-

1. Will you be accepting Credit Card payments and if so, what kinds?

2. Will you be accepting Debit Card payments and if so, how?

3. Likely you will need to make arrangements for cash purchases. (Check the next chapter for more details)

So, let's take a look at the range of options available to accept Credit Card Payments.

I personally use the Square reader. What is it? Square is a payment handler similar to Visa & MasterCard with much lower handling costs. At the back of the book, you will find my blog post on the costs & pros/cons of using square. Please note, I am simply a person who uses this system and finds it very user friendly.

At most office supply stores there are a range of payment options and dongles available. The two most popular in Australia are:

- Square
- Paypal

Of course, you can also hire a mobile payment device, but unless you are transacting a lot of business, they probably aren't very cost effective.

You also need to check and see what kinds of cards they can accept. I did find that with the square I can't accept chipless Debit Cards.

Make sure if you're only going to accept cash you know the location of the nearest ATM's because chances are, you're buyer is going to be out of cash by the time they get to you.

I also like to have a sign on the front of my table that announces I offer Card Payments. Some of the payment systems offer free cardboard tents to those who use their system.

If you're offering pre-orders consider how you will accept payment. With pre-orders it is better to receive the payment in advance of the event, so you won't need to be sorting out payments on the day!

If you intend to use any payment system that requires an online facility:

1. Check during your set up that it works
2. Make sure your pricing modules are set up at least several days in advance with any amended pricing.

4 / ACCEPTING CASH

Yes, this seems like such a basic question and yet it really needs to be discussed as it's something I get asked a lot!

Readers will invariably come up with a $50 note to buy a $12.50 item. So you need to allow sufficient cash in your tin to make change from a $100 note, a $50 note and a $20 note.

You need to consider the price of your titles too... If you have a $12.50 title, then make sure you have lots of 50 cent pieces. Nothing is more annoying than trying to change notes with other authors during a signing. (And yes, it does happen!)

I like to have a paper inside my tin showing the breakdown of coin and notes, and I always include $10 & $5 notes, a large amount of $2 and $1 coins and price my books to have full dollar amounts, so I'm not mucking around with 50c pieces.

On that note, I find it easier to price my titles at round dollars—this avoids a lot of issues with coin!

Also, if readers are buying more than one book and your maths isn't strong, make sure you pack a calculator that is reliable. Check the battery in the week before the signing. Nothing is more embarrassing that making incorrect change and being called on it in front of readers.

> KEEP YOUR TIN OUT OF SIGHT! Yes, I know it seems like a basic thing to say, but you'd be surprised how many authors lose their takings because they were lax with the security of their funds.

5 / HOW MUCH FOR A BOOK?

This is personal and to be honest, as with anything, there is a lot that goes into working out how much you're going to charge.

I work with a full cost recovery concept. I keep track of what every title costs me, from the ISBN through to the percentage of the cost of my Vellum program.

Each book is allocated an amount that I need to recover in order to break even and work out the amount I need to price at.

I also split the price of my ebook costs away from the cost of my print, as realistically, print isn't as popular except at these events.

So, working out what split you're happy to recoup from the signing event. Add that percentage of costs toward the cost of the creation of your print book.

Then price according to that.

> It's not an exact science, unfortunately, but the price of your print book should go some way toward offsetting the total production costs.

6 / HOW MANY OF YOUR TITLES TO BRING?

THIS IS A PERENNIAL PROBLEM. Depending on the kind of event, you may need to allocate a chair and a table. You may need to arrange for table cloth... But these basics pale into insignificance beside the question of *"How May Books"*.

If I've been asked this once, I've been asked a thousand times.

To be honest there is no one single way of calculating the number of copies you need to have on hand. It depends on how you're getting the titles there...

1. Will you be mailing/shipping them ahead and need to get them back after the event?

2. How many copies can you realistically afford to take?

3. How well known you are and if you've been inundated with pre-orders.

If you're a NYT or USA Today with a massive following you're going to obviously need more than a an unknown author.

Sadly, I can't offer any insight on this matter as it's incredibly personal and does come down, somewhat to what you can afford and carry as much as how many you think you can sell. You will also need to factor in any pre-orders you might have received.

> For myself, for a large event with 2 days or more, I'd be allowing up to 50 of my latest release, then decreasing amounts of other titles. My aim is to get those books re-homed, so for me the pricing is just as important as the look, layout of my table and the ease of purchase.

7 / ORGANISATION... YES IT MATTERS

I SUBSCRIBE to the theory of being organise. It keeps me on track. But what does that mean?

I have boxes of items, tagged Promotional & Market. In each of the boxes I have the items I need for separate occasions. The market box carries my everyday needed items for signing events, including payment equipment, chargers, cash tin, shopping bags and business cards.

The Promotional carries the majority of the promotional items I carry.

Promotional Items include:
Sleep Masks
Rubber Android phone stands
Badges etc.,

I do this because by keeping things organised it makes it easier to pack, to see what should be in them etc.,

This is where I place any completed pre-orders and the goody bags I include, the author supplies I carry (the ones for sale and pre-sold) and even my banners.

A word to the wise, check your supply of business cards,

flyers, book marks, tape, bags etc., at least 1 month in advance. The reason for this is twofold.

1. If your items don't turn up in time, you've got a problem.

2. If there is an issue with your items, same problem applies!

I would also suggest doing this with ordering copies of your titles. Although it seems a problem to have to order your copies 6/8 weeks in advance, all it takes is damaged books, shipping issues or uncooperative weather and your books won't be at the signing—a serious issue for a signing author.

I also keep my banners—2 pull up and one hanging banner in the same location as my boxes.

I know lots of authors who, flustered and fretting, have misplaced these items in the week leading up to a signing. They lose them (and honestly—some of these don't take up a lot of space!) and have to turn up without the item.

Make your life simple! Pop these all important items together if you can.

My personal set up is a cupboard in my office, boxed and items sitting with them. Things too big can be placed in the hanging section so they're out of the way but still easy to find.

> THE LAST THING I love to include is a check list. This means that I can check what goes in to the box and what returns, I can see at a glance what is expended and needs replacing too. No wasted time running around filling the spots of what's missing!

8 / PROMOTIONAL ITEMS AND SWAG

Promotional items are the things authors love to hate. We spend lots and lots of $$ on these items yet how much thought goes into what we have?

1st rule of thumb—does it somehow seem to be connected to your brand? I love androids, badges etc., I know other authors who do scented candles and another lot who are known for their condoms! Most of them write erotica, or erotic romance so it works.

What genre do you write? If you're a YA author consider biscuits/cookies/jewellery etc

I get a lot of items from aliexpress www.aliexpress.com because the items are inexpensive, but you do get what you're paying for.

Other sites worth checking are ebay.com.au and etsy.com other authors use sites that specialise in author promotional supplies ranging from

bookmarks to keyrings. The only piece of advice I would give is consider if you really gain benefit, think about the cost and the connection to what you write.

Oh, and everyone likes a pen or three!

For badges, I personally use patch-emblem.com but a quick search may bring up others you can use.

2. Business Cards are the staple of every author: I use Vistaprint.com.au and have created my own design in canva.com however, it's worth checking the prices. If you use vista print check for a coupon code to keep those prices down.

The same with bookmarks. I created my designs for postcards and uploaded them to vista print and use a scrapbooking cutter to slice them. Depending on the size of the postcard and your design will be how many you gain from each.

THERE IS NO right or wrong in the game of promotion - you could create a booklet of snippets (use edited scenes to interest readers and include QR Codes to make for easy ebook purchase!)

9 / AUTHOR COMFORT

Yes, while we need to look the part of a professional and polished author, if you're spending hours meeting and greeting readers, you need to consider your comfort as well.

1. Dress sensibly. Tight tanks, skin like leggings and high heels are probably not the best option. Find some comfortable pants or dresses and shirts that allow you to dress up and down, because realistically those events run the gamut from hot to cold throughout the day.

For women, throw in some pads (or tampons) because it's always the day that Aunty Flo comes to visit!

2. Water. Hydration is important in these environments. The air conditioner will dry you out and while many venues provide water, whether they fill it up or not regularly is always a little hit and miss. I prefer bottled water so I know my glass/bottle and it stands out.

3. Paracetamol. I guarantee—the time you come without is the time you'll need it!

4. Hand Sanitiser—lots of hands and lots of germs. Enough said!

5. Breath Mints—fresh is best and breathing on a

willing reader with halitosis is vile. Be a friend to your reader. Even better yet, get a pack of those individually wrapped and have it on your table. Other writers will thank you too.

Bring a grab pack of tissues, makeup for freshening up and a rubbish bag to clean up after yourself.

Make sure you take a break regularly for bathroom visits and lunches. It's very easy to get caught up with excited readers—they lift us up and make us feel ten-feet-tall, but these breaks are necessary to ensure your staying power isn't compromised for the rest of the signing.

> AT ALL TIMES be kind to yourself during the event and beforehand. Get lots of rest ahead of the event because the running you'll do during them is off the chart!

10 / CAN I SELL ANYTHING ELSE?

Nowadays there is a lot more to marketing than just the book.

Caps, T-shirts, Mugs, Balls... you name it!

There is no reason why you cannot and should not market those items at signings, unless the organisers expressly place in their terms and conditions you can't. One caveat that I would add however is:

Use quality images that you have paid or have permission to recreate for profit.

Just because an image is in the "public domain" does not mean you can re-use it to make money and in fact many of the images we choose to use on our covers etc., have a limited number of imprints before we must upgrade the type of license we've bought. So do take a moment to investigate these issues fully.

> Nothing hurts more than being fined or receiving a notification from the image copyright owner's lawyers and solicitors that we've exceeded our licence agreement

and are now in breach with a $40 000 fine. And sadly, that does and has happened.

11 / THERE AND BACK AGAIN

Many of us travel long distances to attend signings, carting boxes of books etc.,

One of the best things I've invested in is a fold down luggage trolley. It cost me about $49 from a garden centre (you can get them in a range of locations including office supply stores) mine is rated to 79 kilograms!

I can stack boxes of books, my large plastic boxes and my banners at the same time. This allows me to work sensibly, make a single trip (meaning I'm not leaving any items unattended during set up and clearing away) and it worth every penny spent.

Take some time as well to check that you're lifting using your knees not your back!

If you're an author with a

single book, you may not require this, but as your catalogue grows, it makes a lot of sense to spend a few dollars and have the long term investment.

12 / TABLE LAYOUT - THERE'S NO RIGHT OR WRONG

Some signings are very prescriptive in the layout of your table. To be honest, I don't think there is any one way that works best. The only thing is ensure your readers can see your books (I like plate stands for that) and can talk to your freely.

If you've got promotional items, don't be afraid to display them. Sometimes that's what get a reader to come over and talk to you. This is when the real magic begins.

Having said that, every now and again you'll get stuck beside an "I don't have enough space" co-signer. Oh dear. They are the ones that will either mandatorily move your items or pull out a tape measure. Those are ones you can't do much about.

I've always found that chatting with the authors beside you helps to break the ice in these situations, but having said that, there's always that time when it just doesn't cut the mustard. All you can do is grin and bear it as best you can.

However, practice your layout at home—clear the table and layout your goodies so you can see what works for you!

I like to have my books to one side (that allows me to keep all the e-commerce stuff in a single location—but as I most attend the larger signings with an assistant, they can be there accepting payments while I'm signing. It allows me to keep them moving along, as for some authors, especially those starting out, nothing is more disheartening than the person beside you being swamped and you're sitting there with nothing to do.

Remember a few quick things:

Courtesy in your setup is key to keeping the authors around you happy—a drawcard for readers!

Think about the flow of your set-up: can readers see what you have? Can they easily talk to you or is there a pile of books in the way?

Have a way to pop things out of site that doesn't compromise safety or comfort.

> A SIGNING is what you make of it. Go in with a positive attitude and a smile, because every signing is an opportunity to convert new readers and followers to your titles!

13 / THE BANNER

Okay, I know a lot of authors love banners with bright colours and use the whole layout for them, but there's some basics you need to consider before dropping a ton of money on them.

1. Where is the banner likely to sit in relation to you?

In most cases, the banner sit behind the table. It keeps them out of the way and ensures readers have an awesome view of you and it... But if your name or URL are at the bottom you're obscuring the important detail. However, having said that, if you've got business cards, your name on a plaque and your titles attractively arrayed, if your URL is at the bottom then you're going to gather interest and readers will have other ways to find you.

2. Is the background you've chosen in alignment with what your write? If not, I'd suggest it's time to rethink your plan.

I purchased my current banner off ebay.com.au but there are lots of places where you can get them, including vistaprint.com.au

A tip when ordering your banner

—check that you are buying both the stand and the printed banner. Many sites offer great prices on banners but forget to tell you this doesn't include the stand.

Another place might offer banner and stand but the banner isn't UV friendly. Read everything to make sure you're getting the very best price.

Consider the longevity of it—will you purchase a hanging banner? (with grommets) or a pull up banner. Some hanging banners can be used in place of a tablecloth, others do well hung around like a skirt.

3. Check the length (for hanging banners) to ensure they are compatible with your table?

14 / WHAT DO I WRITE?

FOR CENTURIES AUTHORS have puzzled over this question. Faced with the first signing, a reader buys your book and asks for an inscription.

Your body turns several layers of icy with fear over what to put there.

You look at the reader, wondering just how long you can hum and hah... then you scribble something almost illegible like:

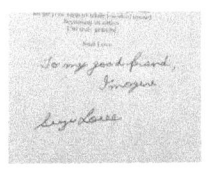

"Enjoy the book" and a signature.

Been there, done that, just don't have the T-shirt! Oh my... So what can you write?

Well, honestly that's entirely up to you. Yes you can put enjoy the book, or fond regards or Don't forget to boogie while you bookie! Most readers aren't terribly hung-up on these niceties. If you're really unsure ask your reader what they'd like.

I personally (depending on whether I've had previous

interaction with them) write enjoy the book and my signature —which by the way, I practice.

If you're a first time and using a pen name, take a few minutes to work out your signature. If you're using your legal name, I would recommend, for safety reasons, using an alternative signature than your normal one. It's totally up to you, but being prepared saves time and embarrassment.

Also make a decision what you want to sign with. Some use pens, others use smiggle pens, particular colours etc. So get creative!

> On that note, don't bring just a single pen. Have a pack handy—as there's nothing worse than your signing pen running dry mid event!

15 / I'M A PROFESSIONAL BUT I STILL HAVE FUN

All too often we're reminded that these events are times for us as authors to interact with readers. A lot of authors take the events very seriously, as business events—which they are but that doesn't mean you can't take some time out to have fun.

Some authors place quizzes on their tables, some dress up (I like to!) and generally find ways to attract people to their tables simply by being who they are.

Take a few minutes and consider how you can increase the fun factor of your table...

Make friends with the authors at the signing too, because these are the peers that may help you to achieve better sales and rankings. If Suzi over there writes regencies and I write Science Fiction, then if someone pops over and is looking for alien boyfriend books, she can direct them to you because she knows that's your genre. Make sure to take a moment to reciprocate if the opportunity arises and thank Suzi for her assistance when you can.

But while it's all fun-and-games, there are also some rules to follow... These are basic manners.

Don't interrupt an author/reader interaction with a "buy my book" line. Nothing is surer to upset them.

Be respectful of those around you.

Be ready on time so readers aren't left waiting for you to take your place.

Don't forget to order from your fellow authors—because as much as we are authors, we are also readers!

If you are planning to pop chocolates or lollies on your table, grab ones that are individually wrapped. Nothing says thank you like norovirus or the like, received at a signing... (not!)

> TAKE THE TIME to enjoy the signing, because this is an opportunity to be the person who has created this piece of written creativity.

16 / CAN I TAKE NEWSLETTER SUBSCRIBERS AT THE EVENT?

THIS IS EASY. Yes.

However, if you are going to take this option, make sure you clearly tell the readers WHAT they are signing up to. Have them fill out the form themselves or display a QR code that takes them directly to the sign up site.

Inform them how often you are likely to email.

Send a "welcome to my email list" as soon as practicable after the event and be prepared for a % to unsubscribe immediately.

	IMOGENE NIX NEWSLETTER SIGN UP FORM		
YOUR FIRST NAME	YOUR EMAIL ADDRESS	PROMO ONLY / ARC'S/PRNL	SUB

This particular layout works best for me. Make your pages at least 2 - 3 lines deep to allow for larger writing or long addresses and names!

Or can I run a raffle? If you are running it at your table

and only for those signing up for your newsletter, then there is probably no reason why you can't though I do advocate checking with the organisers first!

> Newsletter subscribers sourced from signings can be awesome, but take your time wooing them online to ensure they become your greatest advocates!

17 / QUESTIONS TO ASK IN ADVANCE

Before you being, there are a number of questions you, as attending authors need to ask your organisers.

1. What time will you gain access to the venue and what time do the doors open?
2. Will there be breaks for meals?
3. Is there a bookstore attending and can you process your own payments?
4. Do you need your own insurance - the answer is likely no, but checking could be the answer to a lot of legal issues down the track.
5. Do I need to bring tables, chairs, tablecloths?
6. Is there allocated seating and if so, when do we get access to the layout?
7. Is there access to powerpoint if necessary?
8. What time does the signing close for the night?
9. Where is the nearest ATM? Bathroom? Shop for meals if necessary?
10. Where can I leave my bag if I check out of my hotel on the last morning of the event? And is this location secure?

11. Paid or Free Parking?

12. Will I need to tag my books as purchased from the author if a bookstore is attending or will my "signed by the author" stickers be sufficient?

13. Will the organisers have tax receipts available for you - this is after all, a business event.

14. (Possibly the most important) Pre and after-party details!!

Being aware and knowledgable will help to make the event better for everyone and you'll be more comfortable in the lead up to the signing with your questions answered.

18 / SOME LAST TASTY TIPS

- Bags: Yes, bags. If you're selling a bucketload of books (and let's face it, that does happen) your readers need something to take all those lovely volumes home in. (Along with swag!!)

From time-to-time I've seen readers come with shopping trolleys (usually for the free books—which are totally the bane of selling authors) but most don't, so make an allocation for shopping bags to give them a way to carry the goodies. Whether you sell them custom printed calico bags or plastic bags...

- If you need a pillow for your backside, make sure to pack one. Relying on others to have these on hands never works out!
- Some authors suggest splitting your stock and swag up so you have some for the second day of a two day signing.
- Pop some postage satchels/labels into your box in case you have readers who want to buy and

- are overloaded. Some will be more than happy to pay for postage under these situations.
- Have a postage price list on hand. Also know the weight of your books. Either that or grab the link to your shipping/postage site so you can calculate the costs! (check www.auspost.com.au for details)
- If you wear glasses and take them off to sign a book, invest in a glasses chain so you won't lose your glasses! (Thanks to Suzi Love for that suggestion!)
- Don't forget to turn your phone to silent. Imagine 50 phones going off at once… ouch!
- Do take a receipt book just in case you require one for readers who ask.

Don't forget a grab-bag of little items you may need including:

- Scissors
- Sticky Table
- Nappy Pins
- Chargers (including battery chargers if you aren't flying)
- Your box packing list

I've included my personal packing list at the back of the book as it may give you a starting point!

THE BLOG POSTS

In the next couple of pages, you'll find the blog posts that started the flow of this book.
　*Payment Options and the Square
　*Getting Organised

A quick ready reckoner:
　*My Personal Packing List

PAYMENT OPTIONS

Okay so over the last couple of days I've been asked a number of times about my Eftpos facility—the Square Reader. So, because I really like it (no I'm not affiliated to them in any way) here is the down-low on them.

Squareup is newer to the Australian marketplace, offering a reader that you can plug into your iPhone, iPad or android in order to accept a range of payments:

The great thing with Square is, firstly: the amount it costs to get the system up and running. For $19AU you can purchase the tiny chip reader device and get started. **The app itself is free**.

The device comes with a USB charging cable and you can plug it into your computer. Once you set up your products, categories and bank account *ta da!* you're ready to start accepting payments

Happy to spend a little more? For $59AU you can purchase the Tap-&-Go unit plus you get the chip reader as well. The only drawback to this, is if like me you already have the chip reader, you now have two.

All you need is the WiFi connection your phone offers.

...Okay so down to pricing.

The square system is simple to use, and has a 2 tier pricing system. (*All prices correct as of March 2017*)

Pricing:

• **1.9%** for each card tapped, inserted, or swiped transaction the Square Point of Sale app

• **2.2%** for each manually entered payment through the Square Point of Sale app

• **2.2%** for each Square Invoice paid securely online

• **2.2%** for each payment through the Square E-Commerce API

• **2.2%** for each Virtual Terminal payment

Fees	Bendigo	St. George	BankWest	NAB	Commonwealth Bank of Australia	Westpac	ANZ
Setup	$195	$275	$575	$80	$484	$110	$99
Annual	-	-	-	$28	-	-	$30
Monthly	$40	$55	$30	$7	$44	$20	$40
Transaction Fee	-1.8%	2.75%	1.69% + 13c	0.8%-1.2%	1.65% + 28c or $22/month	1%-3%	4.9% pr $50/month
Exit Fee	$250 < 12mth	-	-	$150	$110	-	-

I know other authors who use and swear by the Paypal reader, though for me a part of the attraction of the square reader is the initial cost to set up and the ongoing fees are generally lower using the Square Reader.

*There is no cost for getting the PayPal Here app, and the card reader is just $99 now. You simply pay 1.95% for transactions through the card reader and PayPal check-in payments, and 2.9% + **$0.30** for Key in card payments. Cash transactions will be added to your PayPal account free of charge.*

Another big positive for me is the size of the reader itself. It's small enough to fit in your handbag, lightweight and that makes it awesome for authors lugging boxes of books, swag and even pre-orders to conferences, conventions and even markets!

Once you get inside the app, which is accessed online, you find the site is super easy to use.

Simply you set up your account—you will need your bank details on hand, your ABN if you have one and address/telephone number.

I set mine up in 5 minutes. Then I started on the items themselves. They aren't tricky and you can have multiple pricing for each item. I included a conference price and a regular, which is the one I use on my website for sales where the customer needs to contact me.

I can track my stock, add AU postage if I need to—and I have, to make life simple—I've already added my surcharge into the costing.

<u>A note about surcharges:</u>

The RBA (Reserve Bank of Australia) hasn't set an amount for the permitted surcharge amount, but they have defined which costs will be allowed to be included in the allowable surcharge. The actual cost of a transaction does not include the costs of accepting card payments in general (e.g. costs involved in the risk of fraud, or IT infrastructure).
Canstar.com.au

If you plan to add the surcharge, you need that somewhere on your signage. I do mine by stating "1.9% surcharge included" and only charge that across the board.

And Receipting?

Okay the reality is that these affairs are generally considered to be markets. So rule of thumb is YOU DON'T NEED to receipt every items, however, the Square Reader has that under control too! Your customer, at the time of entering their details (pin etc) can choose to receive a receipt via email. The great thing is, it itemises everything, so if they want a full list, it's there!

The Square Reader are available from Officeworks, Bunnings, Apple Stores and through their website www.squareup.com.

GETTING ORGANISED

It's funny, I sit here now and consider myself, if not an old hand, then at least a more than a novice in the Signing Event world.

Today I was talking to a newer author, and shared my set-up organisation list. It occurred to me, others might benefit from it too.

So, when packing for a signing, this is what I box up. Now the numbers of items are fluid, but it gives you a bit of an insight into how I prepare.

Signing Event Set-Up List:
Finances:
Money tin
Cash Float—minimum $50 in mixed coin and note
Eftpos—Square Reader (or your alternative)
Phone & iPad with charger and extension cord if near a power point.
Payment Accepted sign

Layout:
> Banner (if space allows)
> Table Cloth (unless I know there will be one there)
> Stands for each book
> Bookmarks
> Postcards
> Business Cards.
> Stand for Bookmarks and Postcards
> Stand for business cards

The important stuff:
> Books
> Signed By The Author Stickers
> Swag
> My signing pen (plus at least 1 or two spares)

The other stuff you shouldn't leave home without:
> Plastic Bags (for readers when they buy a book)
> Pre-Orders—pre-packaged with goodie bags
> Sticky Tape (Clear packing tape is the best because then you can reseal your boxes)
> Scissors
> Blu-Tack

Okay, so it's not quite exhaustive and this year I'm planning on buying a trolley to carry everything. It will make my life easier, knowing I can print out this list, tick everything off and take it with me.

Oh and while I think about it... remember, if your boxes are being stored, write your NAME and DO NOT DESTROY on them, otherwise, they get crushed and thrown out, making the trip back home a little more difficult.

Hope that helps with the planning!

MY PERSONAL PACKING LIST:

This document is meant only as a starting point—I tend to have this printed and laminated and adhered to the top of my 'Market box'.

This allows me to track what I'm running out of, what I should have and keeps me on my toes.

Feel free to print this out, to copy or to reword as you wish!

Now you're armed and dangerous, go forth and have fun with your signing activities.

Oh and don't forget to tell your friends to purchase this book in time for their first signing!

Ciara Cave/Imogene Nix

48 / MY PERSONAL PACKING LIST:

Packing List:

Finances:
Money tin
Cash Float - $50 in mixed coin and note minimum
Eftpos - Square Reader/charger base
Phone & iPad with charger and extension cord if near a power point.
Payment Accepted sign

Inwards   Outwards

Layout:
Banner/s (if space allows)
string if needed for hanging banner
Stands for each book
Display tabs for inside standing books
Pre Printed Price List in Frame (1 or 2 depending on space)
Bookmarks
Postcards
Business Cards.
Stand for Bookmarks and Postcards
Stand for business cards
Ipad/Iphone (plus charger)
Newsletter Sign Up Sheets (on board) & multiple pens

Inwards   Outwards

The important stuff:
Books
Signed By The Author Stickers
Swag
My signing pen (plus at least 1 or two spares)

Inwards   Outwards

The other stuff:
Plastic Bags (for readers when they buy a book)
Pre Orders-pre packaged with goodie bags
Sticky Tape (Clear Packing Tape is the best because then you can re-seal your boxes)
Scissors
Blue Tack
Rubbish bag
Minties (for throughout the day)

Inwards   Outwards

ABOUT THE AUTHOR

Ciara Cave is the alternate ego of Imogene Nix, multi-published author and experienced book signer. She's published over 25 books both traditionally and self published and regularly helps new authors to find their feet in a competitive publishing world.

To find out more about her you can visit www.imogenenix.net or follow the links below.

www.ciaracave.weebly.com

*ALSO BY CIARA CAVE &
IMOGENE NIX*

As Ciara Cave

As Imogene Nix

Warriors of the Elector

- Star of Ishtar
- Starline
- Starfire
- Star of the Fleet
- Starburst
- The Star of Eternity

The Star of Ishtar & Starline - Print

Starfire & Star of the Fleet - Print

Starburst & The Star of Eternity - Print

Blood Secrets

- The Blood Bride
- The Illuminated Witch
- The Sorcerer's Touch

Reunion Trilogy

- War's End
- The Assassin
- Executing Justice

The Reunion Trilogy in Paperback

Sex Love & Aliens

- Tangled Webs
- False Webs
- Covert Webs

21st Testing Protocol

- Cyborg: Redux (December 2017)
- Children Of A Greater Evil (2018)

Single Titles

The Chocolate Affair

A Sapphire for Karina

BioCybe

Hesparia's Tears

Tomorrow's Promise

A Bar In Paris

Blame The Wine

A Stranger's Embrace

Revenge On Cupid

Inheritance Of The Blood

The Plan

Loving Memories (2018)

Non Fiction

Self Publishing: Absolute Beginners Guide (With Suzi Love)

www.ingramcontent.com/pod-product-compliance
Lightning Source LLC
Chambersburg PA
CBHW070312010526
44107CB00056B/2570